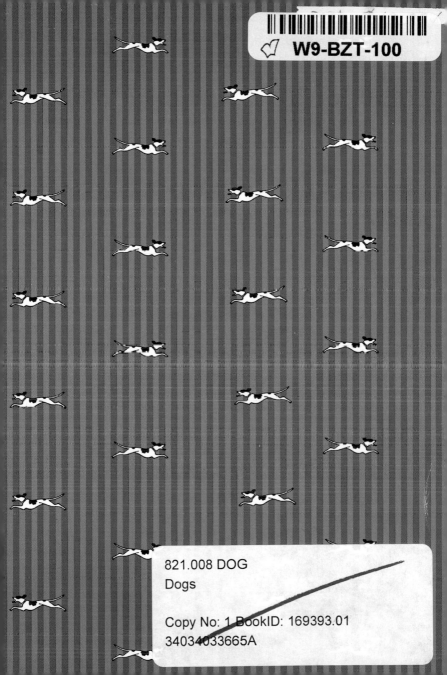

Originally published in the United States by Chronicle Books.
First published in Great Britain in 1992 by
PAVILION BOOKS LIMITED
196 Shaftesbury Avenue, London WC2H 8JL

ISBN: 1-85145-913-8

A CIP catalogue record for this book is available
from the British Library

2 4 6 8 10 9 7 5 3 1

Printed in Hong Kong

PICTURE CREDITS:
Cover: *Anonymous, 1890's;* Title page: *Anonymous, 1890's;*
facing the Table of Contents: *Anonymous, 1890's;*
Back cover: *Anonymous, n. d.*

ACKNOWLEDGEMENTS

We thank the following for permission to use these poems: "Pete at the Seashore," from
The Lives and Times of Archy and Mehitabel by Don Marquis. Copyright 1927, 1930, 1933,
1935, 1950 by Doubleday, a division of Bantam, Doubleday, Dell Publishing Group,
Inc. Used by permission of Doubleday, a division of Bantam, Doubleday, Dell Publish-
ing Group, Inc. Octopus Children's Publishing, for permission to use "The Hairy
Dog," by Herbert Asquith, from *Pillicock Hill* (William Heinemann Ltd.). "Mick," copy-
right James Reeves from *The Wandering Moon and Other Poems* (Puffin Books) by James
Reeves. Reprinted by Permission of The James Reeves Estate. "A Boy and a Pup" from
The Laughing Muse by Arthur Guiterman. Selection reprinted by permission of Harper-
Collins Publishers. Reprinted by permission of Curtis Brown, Ltd. Little, Brown, and
Company for "An Introduction to Dogs" by Ogden Nash, from *I'm a Stranger Here
Myself.* Copyright 1936, 1938 by Ogden Nash. "Full of the Moon" from *Dogs and Dra-
gons, Trees & Dreams* by Karla Kuskin. Copyright 1980 Karla Kuskin. Selection reprinted
by permission of HarperCollins Publishers. "To Sup Like a Pup" from *I Would Like to Be
a Pony* by Dorothy Baruch. Permission granted by Bertha Klausner International Liter-
ary Agency, Inc.

A Classic Illustrated Treasury

DOGS

Table of Contents

—anonymous, 1934

PETE AT THE SEASHORE

i ran along the yellow sand
and made the sea gulls fly
i chased them down the waters edge
i chased them up the sky

i ran so hard i ran so fast
i left the spray behind
i chased the flying flecks of foam
and i outran the wind

an airplane sailing overhead
climbed when it heard me bark
i yelped and leapt right at the sun
until the sky grew dark

some little children on the beach
threw sticks and ran with me
o master let us go again
and play beside the sea

pete the pup

–Don Marquis

–Henrick Goltzius, 1597

THE FIRST FRIEND

When the Man waked up he said,
"What is Wild Dog doing here?"
And the Woman said,
"His name is not Wild Dog any more,
but the First Friend,
because he will be our friend
for always and always and always."

–Rudyard Kipling

THE HAIRY DOG

My dog's so furry I've not seen
His face for years and years:
His eyes are buried out of sight,
I only guess his ears.

When people ask me for his breed,
I do not know or care:
He has the beauty of them all
Hidden beneath his hair.

—Herbert Asquith

—Edwin Noble, 1909

-Cecil Aldin, 1913

BUM

He's a little dog, with a stubby tail,
    And a moth-eaten coat of tan,
And his legs are short, of the wabbly sort;
    I doubt if they ever ran;
And he howls at night, while in broad daylight
    He sleeps like a bloomin' log,
And he likes the food of the gutter breed;
    He's a most irregular dog.

I call him Bum, and in total sum
    He's all that his name implies,
For he's just a tramp with a highway stamp
    That culture cannot disguise;
And his friends, I've found, in the streets abound,
    Be they urchins or dogs or men;
Yet he sticks to me with a fiendish glee,
    It is truly beyond my ken.

I talk to him when I'm lonesome-like,
    And I'm sure that he understands
When he looks at me so attentively
    And gently licks my hands;
Then he rubs his nose on my tailored clothes,
    But I never say nought thereat,
For the good Lord knows I can buy more clothes,
    But never a friend like that!

—W. Dayton Wedgefarth

MICK

Mick my mongrel-O
Lives in a bungalow,
Painted green with a round doorway.
    With an eye for cats
    And a nose for rats
He lies on his threshold half the day.
    He buries his bones
    By the rockery stones,
And never, oh never, forgets the place.
    Ragged and thin
    From his tail to his chin,
He looks at you with a sideways face.
    Dusty and brownish,
    Wicked and clownish,
He'll win no prize at the County Show.
    But throw him a stick,
    And up jumps Mick,
And right through the flower-beds see him go!

–*James Reeves*

—Briton Riviere, 1888

A BOY AND A PUP

The boy wears a grin,
A scratch on his chin,
A wind-rumpled thatch,
A visible patch,
A cheek like a rose,
A frecklesome nose.

The pup, though he may
Be tawny as hay,
Is blithe as a song;
He gambols along
And waves to each friend
A wagglesome end.

With whistle and bark
They're off for a lark;
According to whim,
A hunt or a swim,
A tramp or a run
Or any old fun.

They don't care a jot
If school keeps or not,
When anything's up,
The Boy and the Pup –
That duo of joy,
A Pup and a Boy!

–Arthur Guiterman

–*Annie Müller, 1937*

—anonymous, 1880's

DOGS

I marvel that such
Small ribs as these
Can cage such vast
Desire to please.

—Ogden Nash

FÉRI'S DREAM

I had a little dog,
   and my dog was very small;
He licked me in the face,
   and he answered to my call;
Of all the treasures that were mine,
   I loved him best of all.

– Frances Cornford

– Briton Riviere, 1877

A DOG'S EYE VIEW

The people whom I take to walk
  I love and yet deplore,
Such things of real importance
  They persistently ignore.
The sights and smells that thrill me
  They stolidly pass by,
Then stop and stare in rapture
  At nothing in the sky.

They waste such time in stopping
  To look at things like flowers.
They pick the dullest places
  To settle down for hours.
Sometimes I really wonder
  If they can hear and smell;
Such vital things escape them—
  And yet they mean so well!

–Amelia Josephine Burr

—anonymous, 1870

FULL OF THE MOON

It's full of the moon
The dogs dance out
Through brush and bush and bramble.
They howl and yowl
And growl and prowl.
They amble, ramble, scramble.
They rush through brush.
They push through bush.
They yip and yap and hurr.
They lark around and bark around
With prickles in their fur.
They two-step in the meadow.
They polka on the lawn.
Tonight's the night
The dogs dance out
And chase their tails till dawn.

–Karla Kuskin

–Cecil Aldin, 1912

–Maud Earl, 1914

DOG IN CHAIR

Aha! I've caught you there again!
I'm really very angry – when
I've told you fifty times or more,
A puppy's place is on the floor,
And not upon an easy chair.
You've made the cover thick with hair,
And left the print of dirty paws,
And pulled the threads with scratching claws.
I simply will not have you in it.

The moments pass, and by and by,
Out of the corner of my eye,
I see you softly, gently creeping
Across the rug, and nimbly leaping
Upon the chair's inviting seat.
What shall I do? Again repeat
My scolding? No, I'll let it rest;
The ostrich method is the best.
Although we both know where your place is,
At least we're saving both our faces!

–*Margaret Mackprang Mackay*

–Adolf Dietrich, 1939

CONTENTMENT

I like the way that the world is made,
   (Tickle me, please, behind the ears)
With part in the sun and part in the shade
   (Tickle me, please, behind the ears).
This comfortable spot beneath a tree
Was probably planned for you and me;
Why do you suppose God made a flea?
Tickle me more behind the ears.

–Burges Johnson

TO SUP LIKE A PUP

To sup
Like a pup,
To gulp it all up
No napkin
No fork
No spoon
And no cup
But to slup
With your tongue
In dee-lish-able laps . . .
What luck!

—Dorothy W. Baruch

—C. A. Tunnicliffe, 1938

MY DOG'S TAIL

What put the wiggle in a little dog's tail
   I'd like to know!
That gay little wiggle, that glad little waggle –
   How did it grow?

It starts in his mind and it runs out behind
   To the tip of his tail, and then
That glad little waggle, that gay little wiggle
   Begins all over again.

The day may be sunny or dark with rain,
   The wiggle is there just the same;
It needs just a whistle to set it a-wiggle
   Or the sound of his favorite name.

No doubt I shall never, in any way ever
   Find out how that wiggle got there,
But I'm very sure, while tails shall endure,
   That tail will wig-wag in the air!

–Arthur Wallace Peach

–anonymous, 1890's

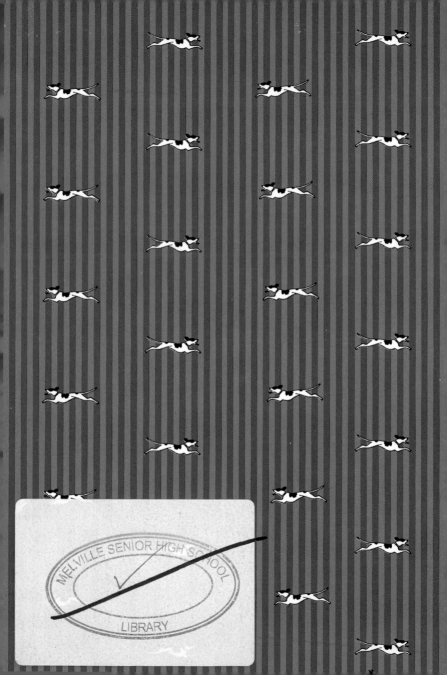